Tiny Toes Adventures Canada

Rafiel Aharoni

Published in Saint Petersburg, FL

Printed in United States

Library of Congress Control Number: [2023916733]

ISBN:

Paperback [979-8-9889547-2-9]

In Vancouver, baby, you'll see,
Mountains high and the vast blue sea.
Glassy towers that touch the sky,
Seagulls soaring, watch them fly.
Snug in your stroller, you'll roll on by,
Past bustling markets, hear the city's sigh.
Rain might sprinkle, but don't you fret,
For rainbows here, are a surefire bet.
Tiny traveler, so much to explore,
Vancouver awaits, with wonders galore!

Calgary's sights, oh what a delight,
For a traveling baby, it's pure dynamite!
The tower so tall, the zoo's wild call,
The Rockies nearby, where snowflakes might fall.
Stampede's cowboy cheer, rivers crystal clear,
With each new sight, you'll giggle and peer.
So, little traveler, snug and spry,
Calgary's wonders await, beneath the big sky!

In Banff, dear babe, with mountains so grand,
Turquoise lakes stretch over the land.
Snowy peaks touch the sky so blue,
Elk and deer come to say hi to you.
Pine trees whisper tales of old,
While hot springs keep away the cold.
As you giggle, coo, and prance,
Discover the magic of this dance.
Banff awaits, with wonders to see,
For a traveling baby, as happy as can be!

In a onesie, snug and tight,
To Lake Louise I take my flight.
Turquoise waters, mountains high,
Underneath the vast blue sky.

Chubby fingers touch the breeze,
First-time wonders, eyes that seize.
Rockies tall, their stories weave,
Traveling baby, just believe.

Mirror lakes, and glaciers near,
Nature's song, so crystal clear.
In this beauty, I delight,
Baby's first, a wondrous sight!

In Toronto, baby, you will see,
The towering CN Tower, tall as can be.
Streetcars go by with a cheerful ding,
Pigeons in parks, taking wing.
Lake Ontario's waves, shimmering blue,
Skyscrapers rise, with views anew.
First time in town, so much to explore,
Toronto's wonders, forevermore!

In Quebec City, so grand and pretty,
Cobblestone streets, the heart of the city.
Château Frontenac, so tall and neat,
Street musicians play, their tunes so sweet.
Petit Champlain, with shops in a row,
Where the river's shimmer starts to show.
Taste of poutine, oh what a treat!
For a traveling baby, this trip's elite.
Your adventure awaits, so take a seat,
Quebec's wonders, you're soon to meet!

In Montreal you'll soon arrive,
A city where cultures thrive.
Cobblestones and Mont Royal high,
Underneath the vast blue sky.

Bagels warm and poutine hot,
In this city, there's a lot.
Jazz and festivals, oh what fun!
For a traveling baby, it's just begun.

By the river's gentle glide,
You'll see the world so wide.
Montreal, with charm so sweet,
Makes baby's journey quite complete!

In Ottawa, where rivers flow,
Tiny traveler, there's much to know!
Parliament's spires rise so high,
Underneath the vast blue sky.
Rideau Canal, a sight to see,
Maybe spot a maple tree.
Chubby hands and wiggling toes,
Explore where the cool breeze goes.
Listen, baby, to the city's song,
With each new step, you'll belong.

In Halifax you'll sail and see,
The harbor's vast, wide, endless spree.
Bluenose II, tall and grand,
On the boardwalk, you'll stand.
Seagulls sing, waves will dance,
Traveling baby, here's your chance!
Tiny toes touch new ground,
Halifax's wonders all around.
For a baby on the roam,
This maritime gem feels like home!

Little traveler, with eyes so wide,
To Prince Edward Island you shall ride.
Over the bridge where the seagulls glide,
With the island's beauty as your guide.

Red sands below, green fields so vast,
This maritime journey will be a blast.
Tiny toes in the ocean cast,
Making memories that forever last.

Hold tight your lobster, soft and plush,
Through rolling hills and gentle hush.
Baby's adventure, in a joyous rush,
To an island where dreams don't crush.

In St. John's, where the cool winds blow,
Baby, there's so much you'll come to know.
Signal Hill's cliffs, so grand and tall,
Seagulls' cries and the ocean's call.
Taste the salt from the gentle breeze,
Feel the sand, and the waves that tease.
Bright-colored houses, a sight to behold,
Stories of fishermen, long ago told.
Baby's first trip, to this land so fine,
Newfoundland memories, forever thine.

To Winnipeg you go, so small and spry,
Underneath the vast, Canadian sky.
Esplanade Riel, a bridge so neat,
Canadian Museum, a treat so sweet.

The Forks await with stories untold,
Golden Boy stands, so brave and bold.
Manitoba's charm, you'll surely see,
For a traveling baby, the place to be!

In Canada you roamed, through mountains, plains, and dome,
From east to west, you gave your very best.
Moose, bears, and lakes, with every step you take,
But now, little traveler, rest your head,
Dream of maple leaves, and where next you'll tread.
Home awaits, its warmth never belates,
Close your eyes, baby, for new sunrise.

To Carli, my anchor and heart, whose love has been the steadfast light guiding me through every challenge and triumph. Your strength, grace, and unwavering support have been the bedrock upon which this work was built.

To Maverick and Myloh, my remarkable sons, you are both the pulse of my life and the joy in my days. Your laughter, inquisitiveness, and boundless spirits have filled our home with love and have fueled my imagination.

This book, a testament to perseverance and passion, is dedicated to you three – my most cherished treasures. Through its pages, may you always find a reflection of the love I hold for you.

About the Author

Rafiel Aharoni is a writer with a passion for kindling the flames of imagination and curiosity in children. He believes in the power of stories to inspire, teach, and transport young readers into worlds full of adventure and wonder.

While Rafiel currently spends his days studying towards dual degrees in Business Management and Cyber Security, he always finds time to create enchanting tales for his favorite audience: kids. He thrives on the balance between the calculated logic required for his academic pursuits and the wild creativity his writing allows him to express.

Rafiel's journey into the realm of children's literature isn't just driven by his love for storytelling, it's also fueled by his first-hand experiences spending time with children. He knows the value of a good story in lighting up a child's eyes and instilling in them a love for reading.

Although this may be Rafiel's first publication, it is certainly not his last. His work is characterized by a mix of whimsy, humor, and genuine understanding of a child's mind. Each tale he crafts aims to engage, entertain, and educate in equal measure.

When he isn't studying or spinning tales, Rafiel resides in the sunny city of Saint Petersburg, Florida. He believes the state's vibrant natural beauty and diverse culture are the perfect backdrop for dreaming up his next delightful tale.

Rafiel Aharoni: a wonderful father, a great husband, a dedicated student, a doting playmate, and above all, a devoted storyteller for children.

www.ingramcontent.com/pod-product-compliance
Lightning Source LLC
LaVergne TN
LVHW072132070426
835513LV00002B/80